STEAM IN THE NORTH

RAILWAYS IN THE 1960s ACROSS THE NORTH OF ENGLAND

RICHARD GAUNT

Fonthill Media Limited
Fonthill Media LLC
www.fonthillmedia.com
office@fonthillmedia.com

First published in the United Kingdom and the United States of America 2015

British Library Cataloguing in Publication Data:
A catalogue record for this book is available from the British Library

Copyright © Richard Gaunt 2015

ISBN 978-1-78155-251-3

The right of Richard Gaunt to be identified as the author of this work has been asserted by him in accordance with the Copyright, Designs and Patents Act 1988.

All rights reserved. No part of this publication may be reproduced, stored in a retrieval system or transmitted in any form or by any means, electronic, mechanical, photocopying, recording or otherwise, without prior permission in writing from Fonthill Media Limited.

Typeset in Minion Pro 12pt on 16pt
Printed and bound in England

Contents

INTRODUCTION 5

ONE
THE MIDLAND MAIN LINE 17

TWO
LANCASHIRE AND YORKSHIRE 41

THREE
CARLISLE 71

FOUR
THE WEST COAST MAIN LINE 83

AFTERWORD 105

Wet stone platforms and gaslights in the Heavy Woollen District: a 'Black Five' hustles into Batley with a parcels train—the sort of sight seen in West Yorkshire for many years. But this was 1966, and soon this comfortable, familiar world would be gone—apart from the rain, that is.

Introduction

In the early 1960s, life was good for anyone living in the North East who was remotely interested in steam engines and railways. In hindsight, 'good' doesn't do the experience justice: there were Gresley and Peppercorn Pacifics on the expresses, and the North Eastern Railway (NER)'s durable Q6 and J27 machines lugging unfitted freight around much as they had done for many previous decades. I won't go on, but 'fantastic' seems more like it. I've written about my experiences with the railways in and around County Durham already (in *Steam around Darlington*, 2012).

So much to admire in the North East: here is a pair of J27 0-6-0s at Sunderland, built according to the old NER's P3 design.

STEAM IN THE NORTH

This book is about steam engines operating just a bit further afield. For most of us, at least part of being a railway enthusiast is looking beyond your home town. Life is different now, but if you lived in Darlington in the 1960s, you had to wait a long time for most of the Scottish-based Pacifics to come to you: the closest they usually came was Newcastle, where most through-trains changed engines and Scottish machines were serviced and turned back whence they came. That was just for ex-LNER machinery; if you wanted even more variety in the numbers you collected or the photographs you took, Southern and Great Western locomotives were a very long way away. Realistically, a day out with something different meant heading west or south to the ex-LMS: the trains looked different, the countryside was altogether different, and all those hills meant that the railways tended to operate differently too—with bankers to get up to Shap Summit, for example, and strange practices like wheel-tapping.

Above: Wheel tapping on the Thames-Clyde Express at Leeds. I never observed this on the East Coast Main Line (ECML). It was never entirely clear whether anything happened as a result of all this tapping.

Below: They did things differently on the former London, Midland and Scottish Railway (LMS). Then again, all those hills meant they had to. Here, a Standard Class 4 4-6-0 drifts back down from Shap Summit after banking a northbound freight.

INTRODUCTION

On paper, ex-LMS services weren't all that far away. The Midland Main Line (MML) at Kirkby Stephen is about 40 miles from Darlington, and the West Coast Main Line (WCML) at Tebay about 53. Leeds, through which MML as well as trans-Pennine and various local services passed, was just over 60 miles away; even a pilgrimage to the enchanted city of Carlisle required only an 80-mile trip.

There was more to it than that, however. The obvious train route west had long been over the much-loved Stainmore Line, with regular services to Kitkby Stephen, Appleby, and Penrith. But figures were concocted to demonstrate its alleged obsolescence, and despite a dogged campaign to save it, 1963 saw the end of the line, along with its convenience and fabulous views over the Pennines.

A 9F charges south on the Midland Main Line (MML) at Kirkby Stephen. A fine sight, but it was taken from the trackbed of the controversially closed Stainmore Line….

Cycling was another way to go, though the Pennines might significantly reduce the charm of this option. Climbing to the 1,400-foot contour on the A66 was hard enough in itself, and many intermediate climbs and drops would slow your progress even further. As for a gentle breeze at your back to help you on your way, forget it—you could be fighting not only the mountain, but headwinds both ways.

Hitch-hiking was worth thinking about, but was not always reliable out in the countryside.

Travelling around by train required tickets, which required paying for—an obvious constraint, even though I recall fares being much cheaper in real terms then than they are now. Some railway enthusiasts even had ways of promoting what the authorities may describe as 'revenue escape'. Best to take that subject no further, I think.

There were occasionally organised trips, and I became progressively more mobile—first with a willing but grossly underpowered motorbike, then by car. However, I was only just in time, for British Rail (BR) was moving rapidly, and by 1968 had closed down its entire spectacular steam show. So while this is a collection of railway photographs of that decade, many of the images do possess the sub-text, 'however did I get there?'

As the 1960s wore on, 'getting there' took on greater urgency, and steam traction withered on the East Coast Main Line (ECML) through Darlington. Where A1s and A4s had once been plentiful on passenger expresses, you would be grateful to see them, even occasionally, on fitted freight. Scrapping A3s started in earnest as early as 1962, even though they were performing better than ever thanks to late investment in double chimneys. And so steam's extinction churned on, life for enthusiasts getting bleaker by the day. The Q6s and J27s still hustled freight on the coast, but Main Line steam became increasingly rare along the east coast: looking west to the MML and the WCML was rapidly becoming essential.

INTRODUCTION

Occasional trips to Yorkshire mining country: this is a WD 2-8-0 approaching Wakefield.

Other opportunities to see steam still arose for a while: I had relatives in West Yorkshire, and sometimes combined family visits with a trip to the Calder Valley Line or into the coal-mining districts to the south.

I have written elsewhere about how I began to lose interest in the traditional 'wedge' shots of trains—three-quarter views of the front of the engine, with train strung out neatly behind. Maybe looking at the work of 'proper' photographers in Darlington library didn't help. It seemed unlikely that Cartier-Bresson or Bill Brandt would be satisfied with the wedge, so I launched a quest for something else. There were other triggers too—I do recall having cycled to the MML and back on a hot summer day, and all the toil that this took. After I developed the film I had exposed there, I found I had wedge shots of a couple of Black 5s, an 8F, and a Midland 4F, none of which showed any exhaust in the July heat. The results simply didn't justify the effort.

STEAM IN THE NORTH

A big motivation for a day out in the hills was seeing different kinds of locomotives. The 9Fs (above) represented just about the last word in British mainline steam power. There were a few in the North East, but principally on the spectacular Tyne Dock to Consett service, blasting away with iron ore for the furnaces up in the hills there—rare indeed in Darlington. The 4F (below) was very different—dating back to a 1911 Midland Railway design and, in many people's eyes, distinctly primitive by the standards of the 1960s. But these are 'wedge' shots; they show what went past, but ho, hum: one started to look like another, and I began to resent the effort needed to get these interesting but bland images. Imagine cycling up into the Pennines on a hot day, and not even getting any exhaust effects after the ambient temperature had built up. Surely there were other options....

INTRODUCTION

The worst of the 'anti-wedge' experimentation which followed got thrown away years ago. When I tried to include plenty of context, the train sometimes got overlooked. I tried to produce an image of just a steam exhaust and peaceful fells, but never quite managed it. And the kit I had was limited, so I had to improvise, which at times went horribly wrong.

Just steam and fells—harder to capture than you might think.

Different options—capturing the movement.

STEAM IN THE NORTH

On the other hand, there were all sorts of ways in which to move away from endless wedge shots. Following a moving train with the camera set at a slow shutter speed ('panning') blurred the background and gave an impression of movement if used correctly; selective focusing could emphasise a buffer beam, say, rather than a cab; filters and longer-focus lenses changed the effects too. The key thing, though, was inevitably the subject matter: what to include and exclude? was 'foreground interest' really just 'clutter'? and so on. Of course it was a lot easier to be brave if there were plenty of steam engines in prospect: if you've been waiting six months for a steam special and think one ambitious shot has a 20-per-cent chance of success, you probably won't take the risk. Prior to 1968, you might well take the 20-per-cent risk with five trains, then five more if you thought it was necessary.

A yellow filter makes a routine 8F image look a bit more cheerful.

The silhouette effect from the winter sun as it sets behind more hills in the west.

INTRODUCTION

Lots of interesting surroundings: a WD 2-8-0 reflected in the Liverpool–Leeds canal, on a fitted freight, no less.

On the other hand, including more of the trains' surroundings—wet platforms, reflections in the canal, and so on—has, with the passage of time, become a trigger for nostalgia. I didn't know it at the time, but luggage trolleys on stations, semaphore signals, and regional colour schemes—the orange of the North Eastern, or maroon of the London Midland—were almost as endangered as the dwindling stock of steam engines themselves.

STEAM IN THE NORTH

Adding more context, the weather could be absolutely dreadful. Yes, that is ice on the water tower as the 9F sets out.

Capturing the more complex images which surrounded the steam engine in its heyday wasn't always easy. If you tried to show the billowing clouds left by a lightly-worked Britannia on a rainy day, say, you had to be careful to capture some sight of the locomotive, for all that steam was capable of taking over the whole shot. Then take the other image on this page, the 9F setting out along the MML in very wintry conditions: just witnessing the marvellous, noisy, and almost violent event as the powerful locomotive was pitted against the elements was a priviledge. But there were crucial decisions to make. What to focus on? (the still-warm brazier looks interesting, but what about the locomotive itself, the ice on the water tower and its chain?) Then there's the whole question of exposure: the light isn't good, but too long on the shutter and you risk blurring the image with your shivering or missing the big 2-10-0 when it accelerates. In the end, everybody needs a bit of luck in these sorts of conditions.

INTRODUCTION

A brief autobiographical note: I must have started looking at trains at a younger age than I remember—here I am with my sister and the streamlined A4 Pacific 'Andrew K McCosh'.

Nowadays, a lot of modern development is hidden away, in many cases as part of an attempt to avoid upsetting sensitive NIMBY neighbours. There are certainly exceptions, but it looks as if people thought differently back when railways were first built—particularly in the North of England, where in lots of places you cannot easily miss the railway and its accessories. Think how dull much of the British landscape would be without these rails and embankments. This is a Black 5 in Skipton, fussing around with some parcels vans.

STEAM IN THE NORTH

We sometimes forget how widespread the British interest in trains in the 1960s was. When Dr Beeching took an interest in closing a line, many people pulled together to tell him not to do any such thing. When he ignored them, turnouts on last days could number thousands. At mainline stations and significant bridges, there were usually little knots of number takers and watchers—mostly schoolboys, of course, but not exclusively so—and there were plenty of adults who could tell you the difference between an 8F and a 9F.

Above: Crowds line the route of a steam special; I think most people were reasonably conscious of basic safety issues, and I don't know of any accidents at all, but I can almost hear today's Health and Safety officials tearing their hair out at this level of serial trespassing.

Left: Trainspotters at Skipton.

The Midland Main Line

The Midland Main Line in its entirety provides an alternative to the East Coast Main Line and the West Coast Main Line routes from London to Scotland. I am, however, only covering Leeds to Carlisle in this book, and I will look at the two cities themselves later. This chapter focuses on those gradients and viaducts and tunnels still used by regular services today. The line is, of course, also particularly popular for steam-hauled specials, with big engines from all sorts of backgrounds blasting away at the gradients, exhausts lingering over the empty fells for a while before the diesels return.

Visiting the MML these days may conjure reminiscences of the 1960s, but the overall experience has inevitably changed. In this section, I want to concentrate on the 'average' and the 'normal' steam train, so there are bound to be contrasts with the current pattern of occasional, spectacular 'specials'.

The MML on a summer's day: the coupled wheels on the 9F churn away through Dent station. The 9Fs had more power than anything else that ran on coal and water, but even so, a heavy train on wet rails didn't necessarily go very quickly up these grades.

More surprising than a 9F making good time was the progress of this much smaller Class 2 2-6-0, as it whisked a mixed freight southwards. On paper, it was seriously short of tractive effort, so I suppose this goes to show what a keen crew with a machine in good shape can do.

On an average working day in the 1960s, the MML certainly differed from the ECML closer to home. To start with, there wasn't as much express passenger traffic—not by a long way. There was the Waverley and the Thames-Clyde Express, but for reasons which included all that mining subsidence further south, London–Scotland took a couple of hours longer than on the ECML or WCML. It can't have helped that the Midland route tended to use smaller engines than its rivals—Royal Scots and Britannias were rated in Class 7, as opposed to 8P Pacifics.

THE MIDLAND MAIN LINE

A variety of wedge shots in summer. There were an awful lot of Black 5s, but I was especially glad to see the Crab 2-6-0. Traditional images such as these motivated me to develop a different photographic style. A lot of effort went into cycling there—surely the photographic results ought to be a bit more memorable.

STEAM IN THE NORTH

THE MIDLAND MAIN LINE

Below: Trying harder in the search for the interesting image—adding a touch more context to a 9F coasting downhill at Kirkby Stephen.

STEAM IN THE NORTH

So for anyone making their way from Darlington to Dent or Garsdale, say, there was a lot to get used to. Not just the grades and tunnels, but a fairly light service generally: smaller express passenger engines, however a handful of the mighty 9Fs on freight.

I have nevertheless decided against structuring this section according to the traffic which passed over the line, the locomotives hauling it, or indeed the important issue of location. Something far more important affected every trip I made: the weather.

It was easy for experimentation in search of a better railway image to go too far: here we have evidence of BR's early involvement in containerisation through Freightliners. They are hastening north behind a Brush Type 4 (Class 47, I suppose that should be). If you look carefully into the distance, however, an 8F toils away southbound, and if you look extremely carefully, yet another steam plume rises from another steam freight slogging away behind. It's a pity that, because I've tried to include so many other things, the hardworking example of Sir William's skilled design is near invisible.

THE MIDLAND MAIN LINE

A summer morning with dew on the grass, as a Black 5 works away on the MML. The birdsong, the countryside, the clear air, and a steam-powered railway—makes it all worthwhile.

There were certainly wonderful places to be in high summer, when the skylarks were in song; or in the crystalline days of springtime, when the views over the fells seemed to go on forever. But then there was the rain, lots of it, and often of a particularly cold and penetrating brand. And that wasn't the worst.

STEAM IN THE NORTH

Yes, it was raining, for hour after hour, heavy and remorseless. It took quite a bit of concentration to keep the rain away from the lens. Stopping it from running down the back of my neck was even more of a challenge.

THE MIDLAND MAIN LINE

Heavy rain wasn't all bad: the wet rails shine out; a small steam leak yields a further source of texture and interest; and low clouds in the Pennines easily mingle with exhaust plumes to add a further layer of mystery. It's just possible to find a certain amount of shelter (in this case at a closed station, Crosby Garrett) which not only keeps most of the driving rain away, but provides foreground interest.

I can recall setting off on my motorbike as a young man one morning, heading up Wensleydale for Dent or maybe Ribblehead. I hadn't got proper leathers on, so as I got higher up the dale, the rain started to freeze and I was slowly encased in a thin veneer of ice. Had I been able to observe myself from a warm motorcar, I'd have tried to take a photograph of the way the ice had coated everything: shiny, semi-rigid, and moulded to the curves and wrinkles in my oilskin. Being the subject of the phenomenon, however, I had different priorities at the time.

I do appreciate that these conditions were not the worst encountered in this part of the country, where some winds are strong enough to blow loads from trucks. Nevertheless, I couldn't see through the ice on my visor and most of my body had gone numb; I even began to wonder what would have been so very wrong with a trip on a warm diesel multiple unit (DMU) to Hartlepool, to watch some J27s.

THE MIDLAND MAIN LINE

More freight on the MML in the rain.

Above: Braziers never looked like a particularly efficient way of keeping exposed water towers ice-free. Efficient or not, here's a tower that has been kept operational. Water has been duly delivered to the tender of this 8F—and off it goes into a drab, chilly January afternoon. I've tried but can't identify the clerestory-roofed carriage immediately behind the tender. Surely quite a way to travel, what with brass rails and an open balcony.

Left: We have met this 9F in icy conditions already. Here, the driver has just opened the regulator and is hoping to get away without too much slipping and sliding. There's a great deal of ice about, but the people who run the railways are used to it and only the most extreme drifting snow seems to close these lines. Photographic challenges? Quite a few, particularly over showing the ice on this grey, overcast day, with a very few twinkling highlights.

My hopes of retrieving a difficult situation before it became desperate settled—to an irrational extent—on Garsdale Station, and the possibility of a fire in the waiting room. Deep down I knew the chances of finding one were slim, and indeed there was no fire, and only limited shelter from these harsh atmospheric conditions.

But just as my spirits had fallen to their lowest and the temperature of my fingertips lower still, a shout from the signal box invited me over to have a brew, a warm up, and a chat. There really is nothing like a signal box stove for generating warmth when you need it, and more than that, a cheerful, all-embracing kind of glow—especially if a cup of tea is involved. I was up the stairs to the box faster than you might expect for a man who had spent the last two hours frozen astride a motorbike. To cap my good fortune, along came a couple of steam-powered freights: pointing the lens through the signal box windows, I got an image of the train, its surroundings, and some interesting foregrounds—all without moving from the signalman's comfy spare chair. The next hour was wonderful: without moving far from that marvellous, life-restoring stove, I could observe steam freights churning hard up hill and rattling their way back down again; the immaculate controlling and monitoring of the signalman at work; and the aura of a complex system functioning as it was designed to.

Thank heaven for signalmen. Thanks to one I was able to melt the ice encasing the front of my oilskins and return to something approximately human, for there's nothing quite as warming as a signal box coal fire and a cup of tea. It's not a bad place to be if you want to watch the trains go by, either.

STEAM IN THE NORTH

It's a lot easier to say now, but exposure to cold and humid Pennine air wasn't all bad. Coupled with the fierce gradients, the steam engines produced interesting exhaust effects when conditions were cold or wet, and the weather often displayed both of these characteristics in abundance. I suspect that some of the drivers derived a certain pleasure in overdoing things—leaving the drain cocks open and veiling their machinery in a white steam wall, for one. But by and large, the hard work of lugging tonnage up to Ais Gill was more than enough to provide a good chance of a fine steam plume in your photograph.

Plenty of exhaust effects as an 8F restarts after a spell 'put inside' to let faster traffic overtake.

THE MIDLAND MAIN LINE

The perpetual problem of trainspotter pollution: I was working away at capturing the departure of the 8F from a low angle, when one of my friends decided that getting a good photograph came down to being on top of the buffer stop—a crucial element of the composition I was trying to set up. After I shouted at him he grudgingly relinquished his post on the buffer beam, but it was too late: another train was approaching rapidly, and together with the 8F would have made a nicely balanced composition. But I was concentrating on the unwanted human interest for too long, and didn't stand up to get the second train positioned where I wanted. Just something else to put down to experience, I suppose.

STEAM IN THE NORTH

I even tried to capture the essence of the smoky tunnels—an integral part of the MML experience—but this wasn't easy. If the train was moving quickly or coasting downhill, the smoke and steam were minimal; too heavy or too slow uphill, and that was all you got.

About the best I could do on the 'smoky-tunnel' theme. For slow-moving freights, there was a real danger that everything would be so encased in smoke and steam that there wouldn't be much to photograph. All of this begs the question, how did the crew on the footplate manage to breathe?

Were there other problems for the innocent photographer trying to capture the essence of steam on the MML? Just a few. With traffic much lighter than nearer home, it was tempting to move on and try to find a better spot from which to photograph later trains. Of course, the decision to move invariably prompted trains to appear in both directions and the light to suddenly improve—just as you were between vantage points.

Then there was what I sometimes thought of as 'trainspotter pollution'. Endlessly dismissive of anything other than a traditional wedge shot, why should fellow enthusiasts worry about getting in the way of someone trying to come up with something more interesting?

THE MIDLAND MAIN LINE

My two most alarming cases of getting to the planned vantage point just too late. For one thing, I have a distant image only of what must have been a wonderful sight close up, namely double-headed 9Fs. It was the old story of moving because nothing seemed to be happening, when the railway suddenly sprang into life—only this time, I had almost missed a phenomenon I had never seen before, and was not to see again. Just think of it: ten pairs of wheels hammering away in the hills. The second relates only to a Black 5, but it was clattering past as I arrived and I missed the opportunity of stepping back, putting on the 105-mm lens and including that Rover (I think it's a P4). If only....

As I have pointed out in the Introduction, the business of getting to the MML was a big issue right up to the very last few months of steam operations, when my friends and I first gained access to cars.

Hitchhiking served me well on many occasions, but here is a warning about what was sometimes on offer.

One evening, two of us were still on the wrong (i.e. west) side of the Pennines on the A66, and had been waiting a long time for a lift, when an old sheep lorry stopped. It would be able to take us all the way to Scotch Corner, thus getting us out of a potentially tight spot. The lorry was a Dodge chassis—hardly a market leader at the time, but I think it had a good reputation overall. This one was in poor shape, though: its engine made a lot of noise and kicked out many fumes, but didn't seem to be translating much of this into usable power. At every uphill climb, our speed dropped to the sort of pace I could have run at. Queues built up behind us, for overtaking was not a real option in those days, the road being a far cry from the wide, smooth carriageways of today.

The cab was cramped for the three of us, plus various cans, clothing, and general debris. Everything smelt strongly of sheep, diesel, and cigarettes. The driver seemed friendly, although we all had to scream to be heard over the bellowing motor.

The driver had a greasy straw hat, gaps in his teeth, and what looked like a shotgun under his seat. Seeing our timid interest, the driver explained that if he saw the gamekeeper heading one way on his daily duties, and he was going another and came upon a pheasant—well, that would be dinner resolved.

The shabby old Dodge took a long time to get to the summit—though I bet it felt a lot longer to the people in the queue of cars behind. But once the downhill grades picked up, it was a vehicle transformed. The driver basically knocked the rattling gear lever into neutral and let the forces of gravity take their course. To start with, it was all very quiet compared with the torturous climb, as the din from the engine subsided. It was not silent, however: the bodywork creaked in all sorts of places, and it was now easy to hear the sheep braying to anyone who would listen that they were Westmorlands and had no wish to mingle with their Yorkshire cousins.

All this time, the Dodge's speed had been building up. It was impossible to say how fast we were going, for the speedometer needle was oscillating wildly between 0 and 160mph, all the way around the worn dial.

One of the Crosti-boilered 9Fs, an experiment to make the most of the calorific value in the coal to raise steam. Not entirely effective in practice it seems, judging by the rate at which the Crosti features were removed.

The MML saw fewer and fewer Midland-designed locomotives as time went by, but the occasional 4F put in an appearance—provided no dramatic speed was expected.

Hardly anyone overtook us on the way up because there were so few passing opportunities and their view ahead was constrained by diesel smoke. On the way down, most cars simply could not keep up. We bore down rapidly on an elderly couple making sedate progress eastwards in a Humber shooting brake. With a flick of the wrists worthy of Fangio, the driver sent the elderly Dodge one way then the other, and we swayed past the Humber like a clipper tacking in a stiff breeze.

THE MIDLAND MAIN LINE

Consistently the most spectacular sights on the MML were the 9Fs on the anhydrite trains from the Long Meg mine down to the Cheshire chemical works. These were regular, timetabled runs and required even these big locomotives to be put to the grindstone to meet the challenge presented by the Pennines. Located near Little Salkeld, within yards of the MML, this looked like traffic with a long future ahead of it. In fact, it did not long survive the 9Fs—the mine closed altogether in 1976.

This was all very well, but I knew the road well enough to appreciate that we would soon come to a kink, now long-gone. It was difficult to envisage anything less than a disaster if we continued at this pace, but how could we ever stop? The answer came through some extended wrestling with the gear lever, and frenzied engine-revving. After a while we were in top gear, and this reduced our speed somewhat; the brakes slowly cut in, and our speed dropped sufficiently for the curves ahead. We were past the kink in a blur, the sheep showing particular disdain for this element of their journey.

As the road flattened out, so the diesel engine finally bellowed into action. The queue of angry drivers built up once more, amongst all the fumes and sheeps' complaint trailing behind us. Two chastened railway enthusiasts got out at Scotch Corner, and came the last few miles home on a United bus in shocked silence.

From an era when there was still some pickup freight, and the railways still served some of their traditional local customers, an Ivatt class 4 2-6-0 undertakes a little light shunting.

THE MIDLAND MAIN LINE

9Fs in close-up. Lots of relatively small, 5-foot-diameter driving wheels were nevertheless capable of rapid rotation. I never witnessed this, but persistent rumours of 90 miles per hour being reached on the whole sounded credible.

STEAM IN THE NORTH

My final memory of the MML in the steam era places me in Carlisle on a winter's evening, not long before the demise of BR steam. I was thinking it was about time to head home to Darlo when the stopping train to Leeds turned up: not a DMU, but a careworn Britannia at the front of three coaches. We quickly calculated that we could take it to Kirby Stephen, get back on a northbound stopper, and still get home that night. The lighting was dim, but with the windows open we could hear every beat of the Pacific's exhaust echoing around the fells and farms in the darkness, knowing this was all going to end very, very soon.

A couple of everyday scenes on the MML. At the time, it barely seemed worth pressing the shutter for this kind of stuff; not so long afterwards, these scenes were gone forever.

2   Lancashire and Yorkshire

All of my grandparents, and various other relatives, lived in West Yorkshire, so I was a frequent visitor. Slipping away to photograph steam engines was not straightforward, of course—'what would your Great Aunt say..?'—but I must have managed it often enough, judging by the negative count.

In theory, I had good links with Lancashire too. I was born there, though I remember nothing of my year and a half as a baby in Radcliffe, and was accepted for a place at Manchester University, though I never took it up—it had always been my second choice, and I had serious doubts about whether my maths were strong enough for the Manchester course.

If you liked Black 5s, 8Fs, and WD 2-8-0s, you'd be happy more or less anywhere in built-up Lancashire and Yorkshire.

STEAM IN THE NORTH

Freight in West Yorkshire: one challenge? How to get a grimy 8F to stand out against a background of sooty Yorkshire stone.

LANCASHIRE AND YORKSHIRE

But you probably get the general drift: I spent plenty of time around the Lancashire–Yorkshire belt, and took quite a few photographs. I came to know and appreciate the sharp curves and steeper gradients in the Pennine valleys, and the sooty Yorkshire stone too. What I couldn't be sure of was exactly when and where I could get lineside.

I have to admit, I sometimes might have got too carried away with picturing the context—not least with this luxuriant rosebay willowherb and lineside shrubbery. But what about the trains?

STEAM IN THE NORTH

During the summer of 1966, several of the Leeds suburban stations were being demolished. In many respects it was a surprise that they had lasted so long: competition from the efficient Leeds Trams had been around for many years—although both were to falter in the face of cars and buses, the last trams being withdrawn in 1959. Be that as it may, the process of demolition left wonderfully angular sights among the glazing bars and passenger barriers waiting for the man with the oxyacetylene cutter.

Through traffic still ran on very expensively engineered permanent way: the scale of the bridge and trackwork it spanned hardly speaks of pennypinching. And all the while, England were pressing steadily on in the World Cup....

LANCASHIRE AND YORKSHIRE

Let's start in Leeds—a big, bustling city, particularly if you came from Darlington. There was a lot of building work here in the 1960s, as City Station was changed around and Central Station eventually closed. I have very few images of City Station itself: it was always busy and, quite apart from official discouragement, it was simply impractical to wander around photographing anything which happened to catch my eye. Like York or Newcastle, it was rarely a destination in itself: I often changed trains there, but never got to spend a lazy afternoon watching them go by.

I have dim memories of elegant D49 4-4-0s heading off towards Harrogate or Scarborough from Leeds and York, or on the East Coast Main Line stopping trains before the diesels. It was always worth pausing at Leeds to watch the engine changing on MML expresses, and cross-country Newcastle-Liverpool trains, but most of this action finished before I got my hands on a camera which could do it justice. So the only images I am really happy with from that era are of the wheel tapper (pictured in the introduction), and the man with his catering trolley, having a rest between serving cups of tea from the shiny hot water urn, or perhaps a Cadburys Snack biscuit from the flimsy-looking display unit.

Man with a snack trolley. The cart next to it looks like Post Office equipment.

Although undoubtedly more prosperous today, in the 1960s, Leeds's heritage in engineering and textiles was much more visible. There was just a bit more grit around.

In those days, Leeds wasn't today's service-based home of the wine bars and glossy tower blocks. A lot of industry was more traditional, maybe verging on the environmentally marginal—like the crane rumbling around the scrapyard (with the arches under Leeds City Station in the background).

LANCASHIRE AND YORKSHIRE

There were lots of Black 5s in West Yorkshire: inevitable, really, when so many had been built, and they were capable of moving all sorts of traffic.

But further afield, things were different. For a photographer in search of context, it was difficult to know where to begin. Canals, mills, flora and fauna—take your pick.

STEAM IN THE NORTH

The canal in Leeds, framed by bridges, wonderful reflections, and plenty of steam engines in action.

LANCASHIRE AND YORKSHIRE

Lines radiated from Leeds in all directions. To the south, you were soon at Wakefield and the South Yorkshire coalfield. I must confess, in the 1960s, I also got quite excited about the Manchester–Sheffield electrics. They were a major novelty in the land of WD 2-8-0s; but there were links with history too if you had read about the old NER's plans to electrify York–Newcastle in the 1920s, the prototype electric express engine (No. 13) only being scrapped in 1950.

My secret interest in the Manchester–Sheffield electrics—at least this one is piloting a business-like B1.

There was continual railway action out in the coalfield, mostly involving 8Fs or WD 2-8-0s in their usual livery of filth. There was some variety, like this B1 4-6-0 making its way towards us. It's one of the named members of the class, 61022 'Sasseby'. The LNER had a long tradition of odd names, many being recycled from successful racehorses. Naming the first group of B1s after South African antelopes conformed to this rule admirably, leading to a succession of schoolboy jokes about 'Gnu' and 'Bomgo', and real problems in pronouncing 'Umseke' and 'Oiurebi'.

STEAM IN THE NORTH

Wakefield. I particularly liked the combination of bright flowers and the WD 2-8-0. Both were flourishing at this point.

LANCASHIRE AND YORKSHIRE

STEAM IN THE NORTH

Heading west towards Lancashire, all sorts of subjects caught my attention—mills, mill towns, curves, grades, viaducts, junctions…. People who don't know the area are prone to describe any view with a mill chimney as 'Lowry-esque'. Yet this ignores the nuances which differentiate Lancashire from Yorkshire—the locals can tell one from the other, even if you can't. More to the point, Lowry hardly painted any railway scenes, and had his own, distinct style in any case. Rather than trying to copy any of this, what suited me best was to roam around, without prejudice, and see what turned up (when I got the chance, that is).

A unique opportunity arose in the summer of 1966. I know the World Cup was on, and I do remember who won. I had volunteered to spend a few days sorting out my grandmother's garden, but this was neither as virtuous nor as daft as it sounds—my first priority was to watch the football. My second: to fire up the feeble motorbike, point my Exakta at a steam engine, and press the shutter. And the third? A spot of digging.

Morley Tunnel, Wellington Street in Dewsbury, Batley, and plenty of other proud mill towns and their stations lined along the route west. Then on to Huddersfield, and Lancashire—only to be mentioned discreetly in the company of Yorkshire people.

LANCASHIRE AND YORKSHIRE

Above: Class 5s in the Yorkshire mill towns: the latticework in the over bridge at Dewsbury Wellington Road frames a BR standard model. This kind of shot was a piece of cake once I got my single lens reflex Exakta. Before then, the chance of getting the locomotive lined up with the appropriate gap in the bridge wasn't great.

Right: We have the familiar sight of the LMS version of class 5. One afternoon it rained at Batley, but this worked just fine visually: lots of reflections in the wet flagstones, somehow all-of-a-piece with the gas lamps and the familiar, functional LYR architecture.

STEAM IN THE NORTH

That all worked out just fine. I made my way up and down the Calder Valley Line and explored some of the Leeds suburbs with more time than usual. There was still plenty of evidence of the pre-grouping companies—particularly the Lancashire and Yorkshire Railway (LYR)—but a lot more standardisation in the motive power than you'd see at home. Apparently, someone from the LNER claimed they had 'the right tool for the job' from among all those different classes of locomotives. I can well imagine an LMS riposte about poor utilisation and an excess of spare parts.

These days, a lot of railway land has been sold off and it's easy to forget just how much was occupied in the 1960s—if not by trains themselves, then by all sorts of other mysterious enterprises.

LANCASHIRE AND YORKSHIRE

Inevitably, there were a few might-have-beens and deeper regrets. The trans-Pennine expresses were in the hands of the Swindon-designed DMUs, with curved front windows from the early 1960s onwards—a major let-down for anyone hoping for a Royal Scot. Indeed, 'passenger train' quickly became synonymous with 'diesel' here and elsewhere.

Daily life at Mirfield. The fireman on an 8F fills up the water tanks, even though the summit is long past, and there's a comforting plume of steam at the safety valves. Sadly, all those decades of steam power monopoly are coming to a rapid end: as a 9F picks up speed heading west, we can see Mirfield shed yard to the left. It is empty; the shed was closed altogether in the first few days of 1967.

STEAM IN THE NORTH

Given a choice of zlocation, I often found myself at Mirfield. For those familiar with the area, this might not seem an obvious choice of location. Nothing much stood out about the town itself—with the possible exception of the College of the Resurrection seminary, but that did not seem to entertain particularly close links with the railway. All in all, Mirfield was perhaps an 'average' sort of place in railway terms, but this might well have been its appeal. Its station resembled many others, yet retained many charming LYR features, such as a line of well-maintained gas lamps. As a result, it came to epitomise the worn, functional details I was fond of in the 1960s railway network.

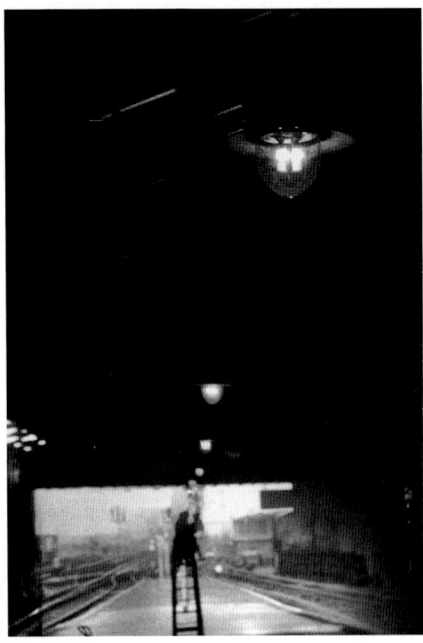

The fine, once familiar details of the Mirfield station, like porters tending hissing gas lamps, now completely vanished.

LANCASHIRE AND YORKSHIRE

Mirfield shed did not stand out either, in terms of its scale or the locomotives usually found there. Services were typically local, and its allocation reflected these requirements. And yet, once again, the efficient handiwork of the LYR was still in evidence; when facing the sun, its sooty running shed was capable of producing spectacular sunbeam effects. Coming upon a Britannia was a surprise: maybe the fact that a bogie wheel was off the track says something about Mirfield shed's readiness for dealing with anything more exotic than an 8F.

Mirfield shed was of medium size and had the usual Black 5s, 8Fs, and assorted tank engines. A lot of coal must have been loaded into hard-working, unglamorous bunkers and tenders over the years. But from a certain angle, the grime was illuminated by glorious sunbeams and mysterious shadows.

STEAM IN THE NORTH

Rightly or wrongly, I went through a phase in which the proportion of the total image which had a steam engine in it shrank. My photographs adopted a 'landscape-with-train' theme, or maybe 'hunt-the-loco'. I cannot explain this approach, and am less enthusiastic about anything like it now. But I have included a couple at various places in this section, partly as a reminder to myself that 'cleverness' in photography rarely pays off. More positively, they set the scene for the action along the track, and show the extent of the land occupied by the railway throughout the nation.

Above: Express passenger Pacifics were rare indeed at Mirfield, but at the end of the steam era, just about anything was possible. Maybe the fact that a bogie wheel has come off the track says something about the shed's readiness to deal with relatively exotic machinery.'

Left: Railways in the Yorkshire landscape, or 'hunt the loco'.

58

LANCASHIRE AND YORKSHIRE

If we continue along the line from Leeds through Mirfield, we soon arrive at Huddersfield, then Manchester. The sheer scale and grand style of the linked Victoria and Exchange Stations made them appear the natural winners of any railway contest, but that was utterly misleading. The emphasis on Piccadilly and the line to London was growing all the time.

Right: The mysterious, cavernous Victoria train shed in Manchester. In the 1960s, Piccadilly looked like the poor relation of this grand affair. I liked it immensely, though some people only saw outdated ostentation and hubris.

Below: Manchester Victoria was once the home of the LYR, which sometimes styled itself as 'the Business Line'. Maybe that makes the 'Time is Money' slogan particularly germane. I expect the lady beneath it would have had a view on the subject: probably best not to argue....

The big game-changer in the Manchester area was electrification. This was not the low-key 1,500 volt dc kit that took you to Sheffield, but rather, the 25 kv stuff that represented the future: progress, a profitable BR, that sort of thing. Like many British technological marvels at the time, however, getting it up and running seemed to take ages. Manchester–Crewe was wired up by 1960, but it would be another seven years before blue electric locomotives could take you to London, and fourteen before the service reached Glasgow. So steam locomotives were banished in due course—though most weren't immediately replaced by electrics, but went through a diesel phase first. As for stations, it became clear that the whole of Manchester's Exchange and a lot of its Victoria station were disappearing over years of minimal maintenance and lingering decay.

I really liked the echoes of grandeur which remained at Victoria and Exchange, but they were clearly past the best of their Victorian splendor, and maybe not the greatest places to work at. A man in a peaked cap has paperwork to sort out in fairly grimy surroundings at Exchange.

LANCASHIRE AND YORKSHIRE

A sequence of commonplace steam locomotives doing nothing in particular in and around the vastness of Manchester's linked Victoria and Exchange Stations. Their monumental scale made it difficult to believe that they could ever be marginalised, let alone closed—indeed, steam engines seemed equally indispensable. But the changes to come far surpassed anyone's expectations: BR gradually cut back the mighty Victoria Station, from seventeen platforms to six, while Exchange ended up being closed altogether.

STEAM IN THE NORTH

LANCASHIRE AND YORKSHIRE

STEAM IN THE NORTH

I am not covering sheds in any great detail in this book, but this part of the world—maybe with the North West taking the lead—had some of the busiest and dirtiest motive power depots I have ever seen. Maybe this was in part due to the creeping onset of electrification, and minimal investment in anything else. But the sheer intensity of traffic meant that there was a need for large numbers of sheds. I have included a couple of images to recall aspects that looked somehow 'interesting'.

LANCASHIRE AND YORKSHIRE

Gritty, grimy sheds—and lots of them. That was my experience of industrial Lancashire and Yorkshire. The elderly saddle tank 51305 is one of the few ex-L&Y machines still in action in the mid-1960s, the remnant of a once enormous fleet.

STEAM IN THE NORTH

And the fruit of a small army of maintainers and menders' efforts at each shed? Nothing very dramatic, on the face of it: Black 5s and others, freshly watered, coaled, and oiled. Ready for anything—almost.

Back to Yorkshire, specifically Skipton—a pretty enough market town and reasonably active railway centre, with the MML and various branches and secondary services running through it. It has never exactly competed with York or Crewe in terms of railway action, but it meant a lot to me because I could get lifts there from my father every so often, so could take photographs without the worry of pedalling, hitchhiking, or ticket inspectors. My father would drop me off and go to a meeting, or look at the merits of some textile manufacturing kit or other, while I put the three hours or so that he needed to good use.

For me, the Skipton railway, church tower, stone houses, encircling hills, and the rest of the landscape and man-made additions sit together in harmony. This has happened without the planning complexities and delays we know and love today. In Skipton, the railway is by no means hidden, but then there is no reason why it should be.

Its place on the MML means that Skipton sees every express to leave Leeds heading for Carlisle, and, of course, all the trains that make the reverse journey. I described earlier how the MML had many fewer expresses than its east or west coast competitors; as a result, it's the secondary services, leisurely transfer freights, and shunting which I remember most vividly. So I'll start off with a BR Class 4 Standard: these were generally useful for lighter mixed traffic, although they were also busy as bankers over Shap as we shall see further on. Then we have the unlikely pairing of what was then known as a Class 2 diesel and a 9F. Thoughtlessly, the BR Operating Department decided that the diesel should lead. It presumably made no difference to performance, but what a shame about the visual impact.

STEAM IN THE NORTH

Traction-changing practise at Skipton. But why hide the 9F behind that feeble diesel?

LANCASHIRE AND YORKSHIRE

Order and harmony in Skipton: the hills, the town, the church spire, the steam engines….

STEAM IN THE NORTH

So we end this section on the MML, though not with the thunder of a 9F on an anhydrite train, big cities, or the expresses clattering down the Pennine grades as the crew on the foot plate caught their breath. Instead, we have a Black 5 on parcels, first shunting in a desultory manner, then setting off on its modest mission to get the vans to their intended destination.

3 Carlisle

And so to Carlisle. Technically, we could look at Carlisle as part of the West Coast Main Line, or the Midland Main Line, or both, for each serves the heroically named Carlisle Citadel station (it's been officially known as plain 'Carlisle' for some time, but I'm delighted to say that 'Citadel' still seemed widely used).

In railway terms, Carlisle is much more complicated than this, however: we still have alternative routes to Glasgow, the former LNER route from Newcastle and the former Furness Railway route round the Cumbrian coast. In the 1960s, the much loved Waverley route to Edinburgh was closed, along with the branch to Silloth. If you go back into the history of Carlisle even further, things seem to get progressively more complex: apparently at one stage, no less than 7 separate railway companies served this relatively small, out-of-the-way sort of city.

The city of Carlisle itself is by no means large: even with extended boundaries today, the population is only just over 100,000, and the urban area within home to just over 70,000 people. I have nothing against visiting it, and indeed have done so on a number of occasions in my working life, but I am not sure that I would make a major detour to get there these days. How different things looked in the 1960s.

Approaching Carlisle: mainly—but not exclusively!—ex-LMS territory.

STEAM IN THE NORTH

At the height of the BR steam era, Carlisle's charms were many and varied: it had two big engine sheds at Kingmoor and Upperby, and the third, Canal, was by no means small. It has to be said that the number of steam locomotives allocated to the Carlisle sheds dropped rapidly during the course of the 1960s, but there remained a need to service other peoples' machinery, and send it back in good order.

All this shed capacity had been put in place to meet a wide range of operational needs, but particularly the long-established practice of changing engines at Carlisle on through trains, both southbound and northbound. Publicity for the ECML was prone to make a big deal of that route's capability for through-running between Edinburgh and London. In truth, this didn't save very much time, and required specialised equipment in the form of a corridor tender. In practice, most trains changed engines and crew at Newcastle.

Stanier designs at Carlisle: in the last few years of steam there was increased evidence of BR standard designs, and we must also remember that the line from Newcastle brought in various LNER products. But when you think of steam engines at Carlisle you are bound to think of the LMS and the familiar style shared by the Jubilees, Black 5s, 8Fs, and the rest.

CARLISLE

Another engine change, and what seems to be another characteristic feature of Carlisle's in the 1960s—a trainspotter running down the platform. I don't know who the young man in the image is, and I suppose it's always possible that he was on urgent business quite unconnected with trains—but somehow I doubt it. Whenever railway enthusiasts moved, they tended to do so in flocks set in motion by rumours of what might have appeared at the other end of the station.

STEAM IN THE NORTH

Crucially, pretty well every train to approach Carlisle was either going to terminate there or change engines. To call it busy didn't do the place justice. Citadel Station played host to continual starting and stopping, light engine movements, shunting, passengers and freight trains both fast and slow, and—let's not forget—substantial numbers of railway enthusiasts prone to outbursts of excitement and unpredictable dashing along platforms.

Getting there from Darlington took a while. I have said enough already about the Stainmore Line to indicate that a trip over this route was both wondrous and slow. Though it may have taken a long time to overcome grades, curves, bad weather, frequent stops at tiny stations, bridges and speed restrictions, in practice, this was no hardship at all. But the Stainmore Line closed in 1963, after which the entertainment value of the trip rapidly plummeted. There were indirect routes from Darlo to Carlisle through Leeds or even Manchester, but realistically, visiting Carlisle now meant a change at Newcastle.

Never mind—let's visit Carlisle and see if it justifies a degree of patience and fortitude in getting there.

A mighty Coronation class Pacific, actually named 'King George VI'. I watched them shifting the major West Coast expresses, though didn't have kit to capture the moment. Somehow, they were more muscular-looking than the East Coast equivalents—A1s and A4s—although comparative tests showed there wasn't much difference in power. The photograph is taken on a borrowed Zeiss Ikonta: if I'd had the funds, I think I'd have liked to have used 120 film more often.

My timing in relation to changing working patterns at Carlisle could have been better. I would give a lot to have been able to watch Duchess and Princess Royal Pacifics, Royal Scots, and Patriots with a decent camera in my hands. I did see these wonderful sights on a couple of occasions, but have no sharp lineside photographs to show for it. The only picture of a Duchess that I like at all is the one taken on a borrowed bellows camera, on a day when I must have been feeling reasonably flush—120 film certainly does not come cheap.

The various Britannias pictured here had been drafted in from far and wide in the last months of steam operation. Nearly always filthy and sometimes in questionable mechanical condition, they nevertheless made themselves useful over both the WCML and MML on most kinds of services.

Citadel Station saw a reasonable variety of action, not just crack London–Scotland expresses, including the ubiquitous Jinty's shunting activity.

STEAM IN THE NORTH

Above and opposite page: Parcels and packages at Carlisle Citadel Station—note the familiar double chimney of a Britannia in the background.

A lot of photographs of busy stations of the past, like Carlisle's Citadel Station, show what look like a series of trip hazards assembled from random debris. These were no such thing. In fact, they were the residue of the parcels and packages traffic which the railways had handled for many years and did not want to give up lightly. Among other things, mailbags, packages, and loose equipment required sorting and re-sorting by an army of porters before they could be transferred to the guards' vans on passenger trains, or dedicated strings of parcel vans. But in the 1960s, calculations of the profitability of all this labour-intensive activity did not bode well for the railways. Some bright ideas were put into operation, for example the 'BRUTE' wheeled cages designed to travel on trains, which kept together all the traffic for one destination, thus reducing the need for re-sorting and re-directing. Incidentally, while working as a not-very-competent Christmas postie, I witnessed some of the undesired consequences of this advanced technology in the BRUTE's low-friction wheels. They allowed one man to manoeuvre the cages with relative ease, but if the brakes were not firmly applied, they were off and running for themselves, straight onto the line if the opportunity arose. So, from time to time, members of staff were summoned to swiftly get the wandering cages up from the permanent way and back to their allocated spots on the platform—not a popular task given their cast iron bases and general awkwardness.

Part of my postman duties involved loading and unloading a van at the station. The most interesting things posted that year? Probably a scruffy brace of grouse, with an address label attached to their necks. And the least appealing? Mailbags treated roughly enough for bottles of spirits inside to have broken hanging on a peg, so that what might once have been expensive, well aged spirits dripped into a strategically placed enamel mug. The only problem with this trick was that, before reaching the mug, the liquor had to trickle past all manner of parcels and packages inside the sack, then seep through canvas, which, as they say, had seen a lot of life. I am not usually squeamish, but could not face sampling the results of these endeavours.

Bit by bit, railway parcel traffic was lost, and eventually the mail went the same way. Road-based private sector carriers were far from perfect, but they boasted a more flexible, reliable, and less strike-prone service.

I don't want to spend too much time on the mighty sheds at Carlisle, but Kingmoor, Upperby, and Canal were certainly a big draw for enthusiasts—almost until the end of BR steam in the case of the first two.

CARLISLE

At the height of the steam era, the great sheds at Carlisle didn't just cater for mighty expresses, there were local services—hence Class 2 tank engines—and all those secondary services which called out for a 'Black 5' on the front end'

STEAM IN THE NORTH

A 9F through a rain-splashed DMU window. The raw power and bulky, round outline seem almost delicate.

CARLISLE

Apart from a trip to the sheds, there was so much action at Citadel Station that I usually saw little reason to be anywhere else, and watched as many trains there as possible. Wandering south meant you missed the northbounds freshly equipped with changed engines and crew, and vice versa, if you decided to head north. One motivation to get out and about might have been the sight of some hills, and of steam locomotives thrashing away to get up them; but the area immediately around Carlisle is basically flat, and in a drab sort of way at that, in my opinion. I have nevertheless included a couple of examples of trains in the wider Carlisle area; the only reason I can think of for having taken them is simply the endless hunt for something else, or a bit of variety to add to my delightful experiences at Citadel Station.

STEAM IN THE NORTH

The first few miles in the Carlisle periphery are reasonably flat—good for getting the engine warmed up and ready for some climbing, but less interesting for a photographer.

4 The West Coast Main Line

If it was tough cycling and risky hitchhiking to the Midland Main Line, the additional hilly miles to get to the West Coast Main Line meant that I went there only rarely until after I got motorised. Sometimes my underpowered motorcycle would get me there; sometimes I managed to talk my mother into lending me her Fiat, also gravely underpowered; and sometimes I got a ride with somebody else. None of this was exactly glamorous… when three or four substantially built enthusiasts are packed into a Fiat 600 D, it's a long way short of comfortable and far from quick. But the Fiat did the job, and these were the last days of steam on BR anywhere, so waiting for better transport was not an option.

Trains and fells—how the steam railway fitted into this much loved landscape.

STEAM IN THE NORTH

In the fells, there were vantage points which weren't usually available nearer home. As well as taking images fairly close to the hard-working motive power, there were the delights of seeing—and particularly hearing—what was going on from a mile or more away.

THE WEST COAST MAIN LINE

STEAM IN THE NORTH

A 9F with a Class 4 4-6-0 banking is hammering away at the Shap grades. If you look closely, you will see a small white Fiat which has brought three railway enthusiasts up the A66 to the scene.

THE WEST COAST MAIN LINE

The mid-1960s were not my first encounter with the WCML. We had holidayed in Arnside for a while in the late '50s or early '60s, and on the occasional wet day it was possible to make a case for visiting Carnforth Station, perhaps slipping round the back of the engine sheds to see the lines of 4-4-0s and 0-6-0s in storage.

Carnforth Station: I never myself saw the allure of this location for filming romantic scenes in 'Brief Encounter'. What were to become the hugely exciting developments at Steamtown were only just getting started in the late 1960s, so their impact on Carnforth was strictly limited. For me at least, this base camp for serious northbound hill-climbing is best encapsulated in the following terms: 'wet', 'smells of fish', and 'functional'—not that there's anything necessarily wrong with functional.

A photograph from the very early 1960s, on borrowed kit and not quite in focus. I have very few images of Royal Scots at all, and this brings back memories of heavy traffic on the WCML: all bar a handful of trains— five ex-LMS and ex-SR mainline diesels were around and about—were gleefully steam-powered.

STEAM IN THE NORTH

Milnthorpe Station, tiny though it was, was better: I recall marvelling at the work of the signalman—levers crashing to send through express after express in the build up to a bank holiday, at the same time making certain the stopping trains and freights were not overlooked. And even more memorably, I recall the hot, cramped, and—by comparison with the ex-NER equivalent—apparently primitive, highly functional footplate of an ex-LNWR Super D 0-8-0 shunting the yard at the creamery.

Photographs from these days are few and feeble, I'm sorry to say. It was a while before I had kit that could handle any significant train speed, and on the downgrades after crawling up Shap, the southbound Caledonian, say, would be travelling at speed all right.

So what photographs do I have? We will come to Shap itself soon, but first there are a few images of the general surroundings and infrastructure.

THE WEST COAST MAIN LINE

Above: The WCML faced years of dislocation as waves of investment have gone into electrifying and improving the track, generally shaving time from previous schedules.

Right: Maintenance work can lead to misleading images: the Black 5 appears to be working the wrong line, but in fact is propelling its train reasonably swiftly along the left-hand rails—in reverse.

STEAM IN THE NORTH

There is a lot about hills and fells in this section. The people I knew who came to these parts to walk and admire their copies of Wainwright's guides didn't seem to mind the presence of a busy steam railway. After all, there had been plenty of time to get used to plumes of exhaust and the noise of hard-working machinery: by the 1960s, the railway had been there for over a hundred years. As the end of BR steam loomed ever nearer, however, railway enthusiasts began to outnumber any other kind of visitor. The only problem with this was, yet again, trainspotter pollution. Enthusiasts were prone to climb signal posts and generally take up any vantage point they liked the look of, whether they got in a photographer's way or not.

There were so many railway enthusiasts around, it was difficult to know whether they were in the frame or not until you had developed the film.

THE WEST COAST MAIN LINE

It wasn't all bad: a lone figure helps out with the composition.

Photographically, the WCML yielded many opportunities for silhouettes against the setting sun and the western sky, particularly on a clear winter's evening. I kept in mind the goal of getting an image of exclusively steam and fells, never quite making it. But there were other distractions: I became particularly fond of the 'going-away' shot, as a hard-working locomotive went about its business. But in practice, the presence of all this steam power—and the knowledge that it wouldn't be there much longer—made it difficult to think of the finer points of composition, and the best thing seemed just to make sure some sort of image got into the cassette before the trip home had to begin.

STEAM IN THE NORTH

Silhouettes against a clear winter's afternoon sky: crisp clear and invigorating, but cold. You could often hear the engines working from miles away, but somehow it never seemed intrusive—just part of the natural order, like the sheep, the birds, and the wind.

THE WEST COAST MAIN LINE

Learning to love the 'going-away' shot. At its best, it was exciting to see a steam engine in full swing, hurtling up and down challenging grades, the driver squinting down the side of a long taper boiler to check the road and signals. At worst, just the slab sides of a tender, with a close-up of some axle box covers.

STEAM IN THE NORTH

THE WEST COAST MAIN LINE

A really hot, still, summer's day on the Shap grades. I encountered the same problem with minimal exhaust effects as anywhere else—basically, their absence. More typical were chillier days, when, even in strong sunlight, nice fluffy steam plumes made a more interesting show—even on the relatively mundane Black 5s hauling oil trains.

STEAM IN THE NORTH

BR Standard classes shared duties with former LMS designs as steam declined: a lot of BR designs were, of course, very similar to their latter-day LMS equivalents. This wasn't true of the 9F and Britannia classes, which had no LMS equivalents; but these were machines which offered a bit more power than, say, an 8F or a Jubilee, all within a relatively simple two-cylinder package capable of standing up to a diet of poor coal and limited maintenance.

THE WEST COAST MAIN LINE

Statistically, however, Stanier's 8F and Black 5 classes predominated, right up until the end of steam.

STEAM IN THE NORTH

Left: When they first came into service, Britannias were allocated to prestigious sheds like Stratford, Old Oak Common, and Nine Elms to work sharply timed expresses. Life became rather different in the months leading up to their withdrawal, when they had to haul more or less anything—probably without much in the way of maintenance or quality coal. It says much about the basic design that one of this fifty-five-strong class is making good progress hauling freight on the climb to Shap, despite having to be worked very hard and what looks like an quite a bit of unburnt coal flying out of the chimney.

Below and opposite: Life for these Black 5s seems a bit easier.

THE WEST COAST MAIN LINE

Banking engines were available for northbound drivers who felt that they needed a bit of extra power. Sometimes this led to surprisingly short trains being shoved up to Shap—but then again, who knows what the driver was facing. He may well have been dealing with leaky tubes, or clinker building up in the firebox as a result of using poor coal. Certainly this was a very busy, twin-track line and blocking one line for a 'blow-up' to build up boiler pressure was likely to cause problems for hours afterwards. Better to whistle for a banker than take any risks. Traditionally, banking engines had been available at Oxenholme for the Grayrigg bank, then at Tebay for the final few miles up to Shap Summit. The Oxenholme shed closed in 1962, but Tebay's remained busy until it too closed, early in 1968.

It wasn't just long trains that got bankers….

Banking engines.

STEAM IN THE NORTH

For many years, Class 4 2-6-4 tanks provided the standard banking service—with no particular difficulties that I am aware of. It was something of a surprise, then, for a small squadron of eight standard class 4 4-6-0 tender engines to appear in late 1967 or early 1968. Again, they seem to do their work with gusto, but inevitably had to go just a few months later (when there would no longer be steam engines on the front end of trains, either).

People who have travelled the world sometimes question why Shap, at a mere 914 feet above sea level and with the ruling grade of just 1 in 75 northbounds used to attract so much attention in Britain. With diesels, and latterly electrics in charge, it's not difficult to take a similar view here either. But

the loading gauge meant that the average British locomotive was a fraction of the size of the machines operated by, say, the Chesapeake and Ohio. More than that, this was (and still is) a very busy two-track line which catered for express passenger, long-distance goods, and all manner of local services. One slow or stationary train can have consequences for those behind it lasting over many hours. Anyway, for many reasons banking engines were available until virtually the end of steam, and made a familiar—and not unattractive—addition to the traffic levels.

The thing about Tebay sheds—along with the houses and the rest of the little town which the railway had brought into existence—is location. How you described this location depended largely on the weather: fells and valleys were glorious on a good day, and dank and miserable when wet; and your experience of fog and ice probably depended on whether you were enjoying the view from a warm dining car, or having to do something about them as a railwayman.

Tebay shed: a busy place in what once must have been a quiet, heather-filled valley devoid of human industry.

STEAM IN THE NORTH

The sheer scale of closing down the steam railway isn't easy to comprehend many years after the event. In 1967, BR withdrew 229 8Fs and 309 Black 5s[1] for example, with various other withdrawals, albeit in smaller numbers, from classes, which ranged from pre-grouping. North Eastern Railway designs through to much more modern BR standards. For 1968, comparable figures were 247 8Fs and 268 Black 5s, and the 1968 withdrawals were all undertaken in the first nine months of the year. Just think of that in terms of the numbers of frames to be cut up, boiler tubes disposed of, and all the scrap to be processed. It's easy to say that scrapping steam engines at this breakneck speed wasted vast sums of money because of the life left in relatively new, relatively modern machinery. Before pushing this argument too far, however, just think of all the diesels that BR were scrapping at the same time. The early Warships and Metro-Vick Co-Bos lasted less than ten years, and the little-loved Swindon-built class 14s lasted less than five.

---

1 Source of figures: brdatabase.info/locomotives

THE WEST COAST MAIN LINE

STEAM IN THE NORTH

The WCML continues to evolve. Such is the power available to the driver of a Pendolino, for example, that there is no need to slow down to climb Shap, let alone summon a banker. To finish off, here is the hazy outline of a 9F, with a plume of steam at its safety valves as it coasts towards Carlisle. In an accompanying shot about 20 miles away, the work of a distant Black 5's crew is nearly done, as they coast southwards on a sunny evening almost half a century ago.

Ghosts: a 9F and distant freight train.

Afterword

Yorkshire folk have been known to dismiss anything south of Doncaster as somehow 'part of the overhead'. In truth, the East Midland coalfields had a lot in common with their Yorkshire counterparts, on the railways and in a lot of other ways. Perhaps the O1 and 9F here (at Colwick) might just point to Nottinghamshire rather than Yorkshire.

This book is mainly about what steam engines you could see on a day out from Darlington in the period up to the end of steam traction in 1968. Technically, you could go much further than we have considered so far. The pace of steam's demise differed according to where you were: if you got up early enough, steam was within reach in Scotland, North Wales, and London, so 'the end of steam' had some flexibility. I'm well aware of the exciting steam operations out of Waterloo in the last months of this chapter, for instance. However, there was real constraint in the cost of travelling longer distances,

and the mundane inevitability that the longer you spent getting there, the less time you had for watching, taking down numbers, and photography.

I'd like to finish with images just beyond the edges of the North of England and the areas we have considered so far, along with some rail tours which I went on as a particular kind of 'day out'.

All the while, steam power was rapidly being replaced. All good things must come to an end, apparently, and this was true of steam engines on British Rail after 1968. Basically, there weren't any. There is therefore a very definite endpoint to the subject matter of this book.

Yet steam locomotives were not all scrapped straightaway: the long lines of dead engines which dodged the torch by the side of Barry Docks in South Wales, for example, were the biggest exception. This turned out to be very good news indeed for ex-GWR and ex-Southern steam lovers. Tragically, machines from further north were usually torched to bits and melted down too swiftly for the forces of restoration to be mustered.

On a day out from Darlington: yes, it's an ex-GWR Hall at Birkenhead.

AFTERWORD

I only had limited experience of Scottish sheds, but I liked what I saw: functional, dark, mysterious—and that was just the tenements overlooking them. The B1s and standards were familiar enough, but there were a few pre-grouping survivors which you'd never see closer to home, including the unusual N15 0-6-2T at Edinburgh, St Margaret's.

STEAM IN THE NORTH

AFTERWORD

Enthusiasts' specials were an obvious and cost-effective way of seeing more distant parts of the railway network. The only drawback was, what really got me excited was not some highly polished piece of equipment from a long way away, but rather, the daily, grimy routines of traditional railway operations. It's wrong to say I have a purist antipathy towards specials: there isn't much I wouldn't give to be rattling up to Middleton-in-Teesdale once again, or in an open truck on the Cromford and High Peak…. I could go on, but let's just say that, given the choice, I would prefer the 'proper' railway.

A steam-hauled special along the Cromford and High Peak Railway. If only!

STEAM IN THE NORTH

Running a V3 and an L1 bunker to bunker has some entertainment value on a special, although I can't imagine it ever happening in normal operations. I'd much rather have had a G5 and a couple of coaches in regular service, but this option was wiped out years ago by the diesel multiple unit.

AFTERWORD

I had similar reservations about organised trips to sheds. I have had occasional debates with other enthusiasts about the length of time you should allocate to a shed visit. If, like me, you prefer to mooch around, trying to find interesting shots from different angles, you will probably find yourself in a small minority. For everyone else, trainspotting is about snapping at top speed, getting down all those numbers as quickly as possible, and then moving on to the next venue.

But this carping has to stop. Compared with some of my friends, my travels in the last few months of mainline steam operations may seem modest and unadventurous. But you can't go back: I'm glad to have gathered at least a few images, and have had immense pleasure going through them again for this book. And that's how I'd like to finish this affectionate review of the last few months of mainline steam across the North of England—and just a bit further afield.

The smoking Jinty is, in my opinion, the epitomy of 'real', no-frills railway operations, in contrast to the brittle glamour of specials. Mind you, hasn't the old ex-Caledonian 4-4-0 scrubbed up well, after so many decades of obscurity? And adding the Schools class 4-4-0 allows me to say I've included all four pre-grouping railway companies. The Cheltenham, too, looks in decent shape.

STEAM IN THE NORTH